OWNER'S INFORMATION

Passport Photo Here

ASA ID Number _____

Owner's Name_____

Address _____

City _____State_____ _Zip_____

Telephone _____

Email _____

If found please return to owner or send to:

American Sailing Association
5301 Beethoven Street, Suite 265
Los Angeles, CA 90066
Phone (310) 822-7171 Fax (310) 822-4741
Email: info@asa.com
www.ASA.com

Return Postage Guaranteed

© Copyright 1993–2018 by the
American Sailing Association

No part of this Logbook may be reproduced in any form
without written permission from the American Sailing Association.

ASA Logbook   April 2021

The American Sailing Association

The American Sailing Association (ASA) is an organization of members from the sailing public, professional sailing instructors, sailing schools, and charter companies. ASA is dedicated to promoting safe and enjoyable recreational sailing in the United States by administering an internationally recognized education system.

The foundation of the ASA education system is a series of student and instructor Certification Standards and Endorsements that are baseline competency requirements of knowledge and skills focusing on safety and seamanship. ASA Certification is official documentation of an individual's achievement and is recognized by many international authorities, charter companies, and insurance providers.

Through its work with the National Association of State Boating Law Administrators (NASBLA) and other organizations, ASA supports the national recreational boating education standards, which are recognized by the U.S. Coast Guard.

There are hundreds of ASA-affiliated sailing schools and charter companies that use and recognize the ASA Standards. Membership in ASA has many valuable benefits including an official ASA membership card, online access and interaction with a large community of like-minded individuals, discounts for marine-related businesses, complimentary subscriptions to several printed and electronic periodicals, and more.

Please contact a local ASA-affiliated certification facility, ASA Headquarters, or visit the website ASA.com for more information on membership information and how to become certified.

The ASA Logbook

This official Logbook contains the internationally recognized Certification Standards and Endorsements maintained by the ASA. Proof of sailing knowledge and skills proficiencies are indicated by a certification or endorsement seal affixed adjacent to an authorized ASA Instructor verification signature. Detailed Student Certification and Endorsement Standards may be found on pages 19-70.

Sailors and sailing establishments worldwide are respectfully requested to recognize the bearer's certified level(s) of sailing proficiency as attested herein. Assistance with the bearer's pursuit of their sailing interests is greatly appreciated.

Table of Contents
CERTIFICATIONS, REVIEWS, and ENDORSEMENTS

ASA Ecological Conservation Guidelines 5
ASA Safety Education Overview 8
Student Certifications 13
Student Endorsements 17
Basic Keelboat Sailing Standard (ASA 101) 19
Basic Coastal Cruising Standard (ASA 103) 24
Bareboat Cruising Standard (ASA 104) 30
Coastal Navigation Standard (ASA 105) 37
Advanced Coastal Cruising Standard (ASA 106) 39
Celestial Navigation Standard (ASA 107) 44
Offshore Passagemaking Standard (ASA 108) 45
Basic Small Boat Sailing Standard (ASA 110) 49
Sailing Review (ASA 111) 55
Cruising Catamaran Standard (ASA 114) 56
Basic Celestial Navigation Endorsement (ASA 117) 62
Docking Endorsement (ASA 118) 63
Marine Weather Endorsement (ASA 119) 65
Radar Endorsement (ASA 120) 69
Online Achievements 71

INSTRUCTOR CERTIFICATIONS and ENDORSEMENTS

Instructor Certification Requirements 73
Instructor Certifications 77
Instructor Endorsement Requirements 81
Instructor Endorsements 83
Instructor Evaluator Certification Requirement 85
Instructor Evaluator Certification 86
Sailing Log 87

ASA Ecological Conservation Guidelines

INTRODUCTION: Welcome to ASA! All sailors have one thing in common: a reliance on the natural elements and the waters upon which they sail. Today, our waters face many challenges including vast plastic pollution, oil spills, runoff, storms, and depleted fisheries. Sailors have a special obligation to be stewards of our oceans and waterways by minimizing our individual impact on the surrounding environment. To be a responsible sailor is to be a *mindful* sailor. This idea will be reinforced throughout your ASA sailing education.

Pollution Prevention and Waste Treatment

A mindful sailor is aware that items aboard a boat can pollute the surrounding waters if mishandled. Spilled fuel, toxic cleaners and paints, improper handling of black water waste tank disposal, and plastics dropped or blown into the water are all common polluters in the maritime world. Many personal hygiene and body products are also harmful to reefs and fish.

Habitat and Wildlife Awareness

A mindful sailor is aware of his or her vessel's potential impact on an area's many habitats and is well-versed in an area's laws that regulate fishing and interaction with wildlife. Global sailing has also contributed to the transfer of invasive species all over the world. Proper boat maintenance and cleaning help to mitigate the transfer of harmful species among states and/or countries.

Resource and Fuel Conservation

A mindful sailor knows that saved resources can make a difference to the environment. A boat's use of electricity, water, and mechanical energy all stem from burning fossil fuels. Sailors are a step ahead of other boaters because they harness the wind. But whenever fuel is combusted, it emits harmful gases into the air and contributes to climate change. Spilling of fuel or oil is also dangerous for our waters and marine life.

Pollution Cleanup

Preventing future pollution is the first step, but we must also ta responsibility for the collective mess that humans make. Sailors can embrace this responsibility if **we return to shore with mor plastic than we take** when we set sail. All boats should have ne aboard and other means of safely removing floating plastic del from the water as well as a spill kit for any spills or leaks.

KNOWLEDGE

At the Dock

1. Discuss the harmful effects of plastic pollution on the marir environment and how to safely remove plastic from the wate

2. Discuss the most harmful and un-recyclable types of plastic and describe re-usable alternatives.

3. Discuss the use of personal hygiene and body products, their toxicity to the marine environment, and alternatives.

SKILLS

Water-Friendly Sailing Checklist - Preparation/Provision

- [ ] Bring re-usable products aboard for storing and serving foc and beverages and for hygiene.
- [ ] Do not bring plastic aboard, but if you do, remove it later.
- [ ] Avoid having film plastics, balloons, Styrofoam, and other items aboard that can easily blow away.
- [ ] Use a large jug of water instead of personal plastic bottles.
- [ ] Research wildlife and habitat considerations for your area.
- [ ] Have an oil spill kit aboard and install a fuel overflow attachment to the fuel tank.
- [ ] Make access to pump out stations part of your cruise planning.

ECOLOGICAL CONSERVATION GUIDELINES

Water-Friendly Sailing Checklist - At the Dock

- [ ] Practice slow, spill-safe refueling, have spill materials aboard, and check fuel lines for signs of damage or cracks.
- [ ] Use eco-friendly cleaning products and low-VOC paint.
- [ ] Perform regular maintenance on the bilge and engine and recycle batteries and worn parts at appropriate facilities.
- [ ] Change your oil regularly and recycle used oil and oil filters.
- [ ] Remove all vegetation from the boat and flush the waste tank to prevent invasive species transport.

Water-Friendly Sailing Checklist - Underway

- [ ] Save electricity by switching off unused lights and appliances.
- [ ] Keep a safe distance from wildlife to avoid collision.
- [ ] Practice the removal of plastic floating on the surface of the water by using proper crew-overboard procedures.
- [ ] Look out for water quality hazards, invasive species notices, and fishing restrictions in areas where you sail.
- [ ] Instead of anchoring, arrange for a mooring when possible for added safety and to help protect the environment.
- [ ] If anchoring, first perform a wildlife assessment to prevent habitat destruction.
- [ ] Use ocean-safe sunscreen, especially when swimming.
- [ ] Use eco-friendly soap, shampoo, and other body products.
- [ ] Sort all waste and recyclables for proper disposal onshore.
- [ ] Use only biodegradable toilet paper in the marine head.
- [ ] Empty the waste tank **at least 3 miles offshore** but never on freshwater inland lakes, the Great Lakes, or rivers.

Water-Friendly Sailing Checklist - Onshore

- [ ] Adopt the philosophy of **reduce-reuse-recycle** everywhere.
- [ ] Save electricity and natural resources by practicing conservation daily, both afloat and onshore.
- [ ] Talk with other sailors, your family, and friends about how to help keep our waterways clean.
- [ ] Get involved with a local organization that is protecting your water and the environment.

ASA Safety Education Overview

Sailing is a pleasurable and deeply rewarding way to spend time with family and friends, but it is also a sport that transpires outside in the wild at the boundary of water and atmosphere that requires your full attention, careful understanding of the risks involved, and preparation for the unexpected.

Boating education is key and this is the primary reason why ASA exists. Sailing safety is introduced in the very first ASA course. Later, more items are added in progression through the ASA curriculum of Certifications and Endorsements.

ASA 101 Basic Keelboat Sailing Safety Elements:

- ☐ Have wearable PFDs for everyone onboard and PFDs to throw to anyone who falls overboard. Throw them like a tomahawk.
- ☐ How to perform the Figure-8 COB crew overboard recovery technique aboard a vessel of 20 to 27 feet.
- ☐ How to operate an auxiliary marine outboard gasoline engine.
- ☐ Have fire extinguishers onboard and PASS: pull the pin, aim at the base of the fire, squeeze the trigger, sweep side to side.
- ☐ Have visual distress gear, orange smoke for day, red rocket flares for night.
- ☐ Have a sound distress horn or whistle, 5+ short blasts means "danger" to attract attention of another boat for right-of-way.
- ☐ How to identify buoys and beacons to avoid running aground, the "Rules of the Road" to avoid boat collisions, mast height to pass under bridges and power lines.
- ☐ File a Float Plan with friends or family, tell them where you are, where you plan to go, and when you plan to return.
- ☐ Stay under the 0.08% Federal Blood Alcohol Content level when underway, both the skipper and the helms/wo/man.
- ☐ Report accidents to the USCG, have your latitude and longitude available, know the number of your mainsail.
- ☐ Have charts, clothing, gloves, white non-skid deck shoes, food, sunscreen, water, sunglasses, binoculars, cellular telephones.

ASA SAFETY EDUCATION OVERVIEW

ASA 103 Basic Coastal Cruising Safety Elements:

- ☐ How to perform the Figure-8 COB crew overboard recovery technique aboard a vessel of 25 to 35 feet.
- ☐ How to re-fuel gasoline outboard and inboard diesel engines.
- ☐ How to operate a VHF radio and the etiquette for Channel 16 transmissions: "Mayday" for imminent loss of life or vessel; "Pan-Pan" if one's life or vessel is in jeopardy; "Securite" for a safety announcement, like a storm is approaching.
- ☐ How to operate an auxiliary marine inboard diesel engine and the electrical, galley, and marine head systems properly.
- ☐ How to read a chart, use a compass, lights and sounds to use for reduced visibility, how to read clouds and weather signs.
- ☐ How to un/dock a vessel of 25 to 35 feet, how to navigate within sight of land, in and out of a harbor, a mooring field, an anchorage area.
- ☐ How to anchor safely and quickly in case of emergency, how to handle windlasses and winches safely.
- ☐ How to stow gear safely in proper and secure locations.
- ☐ How to heave-to for reefing, repairs, rest, cooking, etc.
- ☐ How to rig, wear, use jack lines, a tether, and safety harness.
- ☐ How to extinguish different types of fires and prevent them.
- ☐ How to administer first aid, recognize and treat hypothermia.
- ☐ How to handle a major leak, steering failure, fouled propeller, standing rigging failure, running aground, engine failure.

ASA 104 Bareboat Cruising Safety Elements:

☐ How to perform the Figure-8 COB crew overboard recovery technique aboard a vessel of 30 to 45 feet.

☐ How to provision food, water, and provide shelter to sustain a crew for a one-week cruise.

☐ How to determine tools and spare parts to have onboard for a one-week cruise, how to operate an emergency tiller.

☐ How to operate galley systems safely to prevent spillage, scalding, fire, explosions.

☐ How to operate the electrical system under shore power, offshore in terms of power conservation, and overnight in an anchorage or at a mooring.

☐ How to prevent electrical fires by proper battery installation, checking for loose or chafed wiring, awareness of electrical loads, over-charging, and production of hydrogen sulfide gas.

☐ How to administer first aid, how to treat seasickness, how to recognize and treat heat exhaustion and heat stroke.

☐ How to tow a dinghy safely, how to raft with another vessel, which anchoring technique to use for a given situation.

☐ How to swim safely around the vessel, lower the swim ladder!

☐ How to handle a dragging anchor, boat collision, flooding, fire, running aground.

☐ How to prepare for heavy weather, how to handle fog and reduced visibility, squalls, thunderstorms, and lightning.

☐ How to use a GPS and chartplotter to increase safety.

ASA 105 Coastal Navigation Safety Elements:

☐ How to use traditional tools to navigate within sight of land or in fog if a vessel's GPS, chartplotter, and depth sounder fail.

☐ How to use nautical publications for prudent navigation regarding tides and current, changes to buoys and beacons.

ASA 106 Advanced Coastal Cruising Safety Elements:

☐ How to interpret coastal weather forecasting instruments, publications, and weather routing.

☐ How to use advanced sail trim adjustments knowledgeably, how to lie-ahull.

☐ Seamanship to sail safely in heavy weather involving higher winds and sea states with proper gear, sail inventory, crew watch rotation, and how to cope with crew fatigue.

☐ How to plan fuel consumption and range.

☐ When to use the running lights, steaming light, anchor light, to make your boat visible and signal your status.

☐ How to sail at night, how to recover crew overboard at night, how to anchor and raft with another vessel at night.

☐ How to prepare a bridle and pass a towline to another vessel to provide assistance towing safely.

☐ How to handle a dismasting, running aground on a lee shore, how to use all of the International Distress Signals.

☐ How to handle engine cooling water failure, engine failure in a busy channel or a crowded anchorage, fuel line stoppage, burned engine points, injector problems, a lightning strike.

ASA 107 and 117 Celestial Navigation Safety Elements:

☐ How to use traditional tools to navigate beyond sight of land if a vessel's GPS and chartplotter fail.

ASA 108 Offshore Passagemaking Safety Elements:

- ☐ How to interpret offshore weather forecasting instruments, publications, weather routing.
- ☐ How to prepare a vessel for an extended offshore passage, how to conduct first aid and treat potential medical problems.
- ☐ How to cook safely, organize crew watch-keeping, and conduct a routine maintenance schedule.
- ☐ How to jury rig a vessel in case of dismasting, what procedures to take after a lightning strike.
- ☐ How to provision and deploy a life raft and the dangers at sea that might be encountered after abandoning ship.

ASA 114 Cruising Catamaran Safety Elements:

- ☐ How to handle structural and operational differences between a monohull and a catamaran under sail and under power.

ASA 118 Docking Safety Elements:

- ☐ How to un/dock a vessel with auxiliary power safely.

ASA 119 Weather Safety Elements:

- ☐ How to interpret weather observations and instruments to forecast weather using traditional maritime skills and modern technology.
- ☐ How to plan or adapt navigation to sail under good weather or mitigate bad weather during short excursions or extended passages.

ASA 120 Radar Safety Elements:

- ☐ How to utilize radar to assist piloting, navigation, and collision avoidance at night or in reduced visibility.

Student Certifications

Each successive Certification level builds upon the elements of the prerequisite Standards. Each Standard is typically divided into two sections: *Knowledge*, which is verified by written examination, and *Skills*, which are evaluated by an ASA Certified Instructor.

If the Certification Seal is not received from ASA within 30 days of completing both the Knowledge written examination and the Skills evaluation, please contact the ASA Certification Facility that conducted the examination.

THIS IS TO CERTIFY THAT:

Name

has successfully achieved the following ASA STANDARDS:

101 **Basic Keelboat Sailing**	AFFIX SEAL HERE Provisional Certification for three (3) months until seal is affixed

Date

ASA Instructor　　　　　　　　　　　　　　　　Instructor Number

ASA Certification Facility　　　　　　　　Aboard (Type/Design of Sailboat)

103 **Basic Coastal Cruising**	AFFIX SEAL HERE Provisional Certification for three (3) months until seal is affixed

Date

ASA Instructor　　　　　　　　　　　　　　　　Instructor Number

ASA Certification Facility　　　　　　　　Aboard (Type/Design of Sailboat)

STUDENT CERTIFICATIONS

THIS IS TO CERTIFY THAT:

_____
Name

has successfully achieved the following ASA STANDARDS:

104
Bareboat Cruising

AFFIX SEAL HERE

Provisional Certification for three (3) months until seal is affixed

_____
Date

_____
ASA Instructor | Instructor Number

_____
ASA Certification Facility | Aboard (Type/Design of Sailboat)

105
Coastal Navigation

AFFIX SEAL HERE

Provisional Certification for three (3) months until seal is affixed

_____
Date

_____
ASA Instructor | Instructor Number

_____
ASA Certification Facility

106
Advanced Coastal Cruising

AFFIX SEAL HERE

Provisional Certification for three (3) months until seal is affixed

_____
Date

_____
ASA Instructor | Instructor Number

_____
ASA Certification Facility | Aboard (Type/Design of Sailboat)

STUDENT CERTIFICATIONS

THIS IS TO CERTIFY THAT:

_____
Name

has successfully achieved the following ASA STANDARDS:

107
Celestial Navigation

AFFIX SEAL HERE

Provisional Certification
for three (3) months
until seal is affixed

_____
Date

_____
ASA Instructor   Instructor Number

_____
ASA Certification Facility

108
Offshore Passagemaking

AFFIX SEAL HERE

Provisional Certification
for three (3) months
until seal is affixed

_____
Date

_____
ASA Instructor   Instructor Number

_____
ASA Certification Facility   Aboard (Type/Design of Sailboat)

110
Basic Small Boat Sailing

AFFIX SEAL HERE

Provisional Certification
for three (3) months
until seal is affixed

_____
Date

_____
ASA Instructor   Instructor Number

_____
ASA Certification Facility   Aboard (Type/Design of Sailboat)

STUDENT CERTIFICATIONS

THIS IS TO CERTIFY THAT:

_____
Name

has successfully achieved the following ASA STANDARDS:

111
Sailing Review

AFFIX SEAL HERE

Provisional Certification
for three (3) months
until seal is affixed

_____
Date

_____
ASA Instructor / Instructor Number

_____
ASA Certification Facility / Aboard (Type/Design of Sailboat)

_____
ASA Recommended Plan / ASA Instructor Remarks

_____

_____

_____

_____

114
Cruising Catamaran Sailing

AFFIX SEAL HERE

Provisional Certification
for three (3) months
until seal is affixed

_____
Date

_____
ASA Instructor / Instructor Number

_____
ASA Certification Facility / Aboard (Type/Design of Sailboat)

Student Endorsements

Endorsements provide an opportunity for in-depth study of a single topic and demonstration of specialized knowledge and skills. Endorsements complement Certifications. Please check which a local ASA affiliate for availability of Endorsements.

NOTE: When the description for a standard includes the term "skipper," it is implied that the person fulfilling the skipper role is also able to perform the duties of any other crewmember.

THIS IS TO CERTIFY THAT:

_____
Name

has successfully achieved the following ASA STANDARDS:

_____	AFFIX SEAL HERE
_____	Provisional Certification for three (3) months until seal is affixed
_____	
_____	
Date	
ASA Instructor	Instructor Number
ASA Certification Facility	Aboard (Type/Design of Sailboat)

117 **Basic Celestial Endorsement**	AFFIX SEAL HERE Provisional Certification for three (3) months until seal is affixed
Date	
ASA Instructor	Instructor Number
ASA Certification Facility	

STUDENT ENDORSEMENTS

THIS IS TO CERTIFY THAT:

Name

has successfully achieved the following ASA STANDARDS:

118
Docking Endorsement

AFFIX SEAL HERE

Provisional Certification for three (3) months until seal is affixed

Date

ASA Instructor — Instructor Number

ASA Certification Facility — Aboard (Type/Design of Sailboat)

119
Marine Weather Endorsement

AFFIX SEAL HERE

Provisional Certification for three (3) months until seal is affixed

Date

ASA Instructor — Instructor Number

ASA Certification Facility

120
Radar Endorsement

AFFIX SEAL HERE

Provisional Certification for three (3) months until seal is affixed

Date

ASA Instructor — Instructor Number

ASA Certification Facility

Basic Keelboat Sailing Standard (ASA 101)

PREREQUISITES: None

DESCRIPTION: Able to skipper a sloop-rigged keelboat of approximately 20 to 27 feet in length by day in light to moderate winds (up to 15 knots) and sea conditions. Knowledge of basic sailing terminology, parts and functions, helm commands, basic sail trim, points of sail, buoyage, seamanship and safety including basic navigation rules to avoid collisions and hazards. Auxiliary power operation is not required.

KNOWLEDGE

Basic Sailing Terminology

1. Describe and identify the following sailboat parts and their functions:
   - Hull
   - Deck
   - Transom
   - Keel
   - Mast
   - Boom
   - Gooseneck
   - Bow
   - Stern
   - Helm/tiller/wheel
   - Rudder
   - Cockpit
   - Cabin
   - Standing rigging
   - Shroud
   - Spreader
   - Chainplate
   - Headstay/forestay
   - Backstay
   - Stanchion
   - Lifeline
   - Pulpit
   - Winch
   - Cleat
   - Block
   - Fairlead
   - Fender
   - Dockline

2. Identify and describe the functions of the following sails, sail parts and sail controls:
   - Mainsail
   - Jib/genoa
   - Head
   - Tack
   - Clew
   - Foot
   - Luff
   - Leech
   - Downhaul/cunningham
   - Batten
   - Batten pocket
   - Bolt rope
   - Hank
   - Running rigging
   - Halyard
   - Mainsheet
   - Boom topping lift
   - Boom vang
   - Telltale
   - Outhaul
   - Traveler
   - Shackle
   - Roller furler
   - Jibsheets

BASIC KEELBOAT SAILING STANDARD

3. Define the following terms:
    - Port
    - Starboard
    - Forward
    - Aft
    - Beam
    - Ahead
    - Astern
    - Abeam
    - Windward
    - Leeward
    - Draft
    - Freeboard
    - Heel
    - Weather helm
    - Skipper
    - Helmsman
    - Crew

Maneuvers and Points of Sail

4. Explain and identify using diagrams the following maneuvers, points of sail, and other terms:
    - Head-to-Wind
    - No-Sail Zone
    - Close Hauled
    - Close Reach
    - Beam Reach
    - Broad Reach
    - Run
    - Sailing-by-the-Lee
    - In Irons
    - Luffing
    - Port Tack
    - Starboard Tack
    - Tacking
    - Jibing
    - Stand-on
    - Give-way

5. Explain and utilize correctly the following helm commands and crew responses:
    - "Heading Up"
    - "Bearing Away"
    - "Ready About" — "Ready" — "Helms-a-Lee" (or "Coming About" or "Tacking")
    - "Prepare to Jibe" — "Ready" — "Jibe-Ho" (or "Jibing")

Navigation Rules

For elements 6–12, describe, using diagrams as appropriate, the applicable rules for a 25-foot recreational sailing vessel, as found in the *USCG Navigation Rules and Regulations Handbook*. Identify the "stand-on" and "give-way" vessel in each situation:

6. Look-out (Rule 5).

7. Sailing vessels with the wind on different sides ('starboard/port') (Rule 12).

8. Sailing vessels with the wind on same side ('leeward/windward') (Rule 12).

9. Sailing vessel on port tack cannot determine windward sailing vessel's tack (Rule 12).

10. Overtaking (Rule 13).

BASIC KEELBOAT SAILING STANDARD

11. Power-driven vessels approaching each other head-on. (Rule 14).

12. Power-driven vessel with another power-driven vessel on starboard side. (Rule 15).

13. Describe appropriate actions to be taken when sailing in the vicinity of commercial traffic including responding to a danger signal.

Aids to Navigation

14. Identify and state the purpose of lateral aids to navigation by color, shape and numbering, including preferred channel markers.

15. Identify safe water, information and regulatory markers.

Safety Gear and Procedures

16. List the federally required equipment for a recreational sailboat of 25-feet in length.

17. Identify the location and color of navigation lights used by a recreational vessel of 25-feet in length.

18. Describe the purpose of a Float Plan, give examples of information contained therein and to whom it should be submitted.

19. Describe when and to whom boating accidents must be reported.

20. State the Federal Blood Alcohol Content (BAC) limit for vessel operation.

BASIC KEELBOAT SAILING STANDARD

SKILLS

Safety Equipment

21. Demonstrate the proper use of a lifejacket or personal flotation device (PFD).

Sailing

Rig/hoist/set sails safely and correctly to obtain proper sail trim using the following lines and controls, if available.

22. Halyards and/or furling devices
23. Downhaul or cunningham
24. Outhaul
25. Boom vang
26. Mainsheet
27. Jibsheets
28. Winches
29. Traveler
30. Lower/furl/stow sails and coil/flake/stow lines properly

Without coaching or assistance, verbalize appropriate commands and demonstrate competence, safety and good seamanship in the role of Skipper/Helmsman during the maneuvers listed in elements 31–42. Honor all aids to navigation and use properly the basic Navigation Rules. Ensure sails are trimmed correctly and the vessel is in control at all times.

31. Depart dock or mooring fully ready to get underway safely
32. Select and maintain a given tack and course
33. Demonstrate how to get out of "irons"
34. Head Up
35. Bear Away
36. Sail Close Hauled
37. Sail on a Close Reach
38. Sail on a Beam Reach
39. Sail on a Broad Reach

40. Sail on a Run
41. Tack
42. Jibe
43. As crew, give appropriate verbal responses and perform correct actions during the maneuvers listed in elements 31 through 42.

Man Overboard (Person in Water)

44. Describe and demonstrate the correct actions to be taken while under sail from the time a person falls overboard until safely recovered.

Return and Secure

45. Return to dock or mooring.
46. Secure vessel, using appropriate mooring/dock lines, fenders, etc.

Knots

Describe the purpose of, and construct without assistance in a timely manner, each of the following knots and hitches:

47. Figure-8 Knot
48. Square (Reef) Knot
49. Clove Hitch
50. Round turn and 2 Half hitches
51. Cleat Hitch
52. Bowline

Basic Coastal Cruising Standard (ASA 103)

PREREQUISITES: Basic Keelboat Sailing (ASA 101) Certification, and the ability to demonstrate competencies in all knowledge and skills elements of that Standard. ASA recommends a minimum of 24 on-water sailing hours before undertaking ASA 103.

DESCRIPTION: Able to skipper a sloop-rigged auxiliary powered (inboard or outboard engine) keelboat of approximately 25 to 35 feet in length by day in moderate winds (up to 20 knots) and sea conditions. Knowledge of cruising sailboat terminology, basic boat systems, auxiliary engine operation, docking procedures, intermediate sail trim, navigation rules, basic coastal navigation, anchoring, weather interpretation, safety and seamanship.

KNOWLEDGE

Cruising Sailboat Terminology

1. Identify and describe the following cruising sailboat parts, areas, or systems and their functions:
   - Turnbuckle
   - Rudder post
   - Binnacle
   - Saloon
   - V-berth
   - Bilge pump
   - Windlass
   - Self-bailing cockpit
   - Chainplate
   - Transom
   - Cockpit locker
   - Companionway
   - Auxiliary engine
   - Seacock
   - Through-hull fitting
   - Stemhead fitting
   - Compass
   - Emergency tiller
   - Galley
   - Bilge
   - Ground tackle

Safety Equipment and Procedures

2. List the federally required equipment for a 33-foot recreational vessel equipped with an inboard diesel engine.

3. Describe the characteristics and benefits of Personal Flotation Devices (PFD's), both Wearable (Life Jackets) and Throwable.

4. List the ASA recommended safety equipment for a recreational sailing vessel.

5. Describe ways to keep gear and equipment secure and in their proper location.

BASIC COASTAL CRUISING STANDARD

6. Describe the purpose and proper use of a safety harness and tether.

7. Describe safe refueling procedures for a vessel equipped with an outboard engine using gasoline or an inboard engine using diesel fuel.

Navigation and Weather

8. Demonstrate understanding of basic coastal navigation terminology and practices including:
   - Essential navigator's tools
   - Use of navigation charts and symbols
   - Depth soundings
   - Bottom types
   - Hazards
   - Aids to navigation
   - Latitude/longitude
   - Determining magnetic direction
   - Measuring distance

9. Describe how to prevent undue magnetic influence on a compass.

10. Describe the dangers of, and how to avoid, a 'lee shore.'

11. Obtain and interpret marine weather information; describe the impact that present observations and forecasts may have on sailing plans over a 6–12 hour period.

12. Describe and identify Cumulonimbus clouds and what dangers they may signify.

13. Define 'small craft advisory' and 'gale warning' and describe precautions to be taken for each.

Sail Plan

14. Describe the appropriate sail combinations to carry under the following wind conditions: light (0–11 knots), moderate (12–19 knots), and heavy (20–33 knots).

15. Describe the procedures for reducing sail using a roller furling jib and a mainsail reefing system.

16. Describe the benefits of, and procedures for, heaving-to.

Seamanship

17. Describe the primary responsibilities of skipper and crew

For elements 18-23, describe, using diagrams as appropriate, the applicable rules for a 33-foot recreational sailing vessel, as found in the *USCG Navigation Rules and Regulations Handbook*:

18. Proceeding at a safe speed (Rule 6), determination of collision risk (Rule 7), and taking early and substantial action to avoid collision (Rule 8).

19. Sailing vessels (Rule 12), overtaking (Rule 13), and power-driven vessels in head-on (Rule 14) and crossing (Rule 15) situations.

20. Give-way and Stand-on vessels (Rules 16 & 17).

21. Location, color and illumination angles of required navigation lights at anchor, under sail, and under power.

22. Actions to be taken when operating a vessel in restricted visibility such as fog or haze including adaptation of speed and use of sound signals.

23. Basic maneuvering and warning signals (short and prolonged whistle blasts) for inland waters.

24. Describe the appearance and purpose of the 'Diver Down' and 'Alpha' flags.

25. Describe common anchor types, major considerations for anchorage selection, and proper scope for short term and overnight anchoring as well as storm conditions.

Emergencies

26. Describe the three stages of hypothermia; name symptoms and treatment for each.

27. Describe two methods for getting a person out of the water and safely back on board the vessel.

28. Identify common sources and prevention of fires and/or explosions, as well as appropriate actions to be taken if these situations arise. Describe different types of fires and procedures for operating a fire extinguisher.

BASIC COASTAL CRUISING STANDARD  27

29. Describe immediate actions to be taken when the following urgent situations arise:
    - Cabin filling with water
    - Failed steering system
    - Fouled propeller
    - Failed running or standing rigging
    - Dragging anchor
    - Grounding at anchor
    - Running aground under sail
    - Engine failure

SKILLS

Preliminaries

30. Locate and examine for compliance the vessel's federally required and ASA recommended safety equipment.

31. Demonstrate on shore or aboard the vessel the correct method for putting on a life jacket while in the water.

32. Identify the vessel's battery selector switch and power distribution panel and ensure all switches are in the proper position for getting underway.

33. Ensure navigation lights (sidelights, stern light, steaming light, and anchor light) operate properly.

34. Perform a radio check using a working channel on the VHF radio.

Navigation

35. Visually pilot the training vessel in and out of a harbor, correlating nautical chart symbols to actual landmarks and aids to navigation.

Under Power

36. Steer a steady compass course (within +/- 5 degrees) under power for a minimum of five minutes.

37. Visually inspect the auxiliary engine and demonstrate safe engine starting, operating, and stopping procedures. Demonstrate proper gearshift and throttle usage.

38. Ensure vessel and crew readiness and depart dock or slip smoothly and under control.

39. Approach a mooring buoy (or other mark as a simulation if no mooring available); stop the vessel within boathook reach; attach the vessel to the mooring using an appropriate line or bridle; cast off from the mooring and get underway.

40. Set a bow anchor in water depth 8 feet or greater using correct procedures including hand signal communication, vessel maneuvers, safety in handling ground tackle, and proper operation of windlass (if equipped). Anchor should hold with engine in reverse gear at one-half throttle. Raise anchor and get underway smoothly using correct procedures.

41. Describe and demonstrate the correct actions to be taken while *under power* from the time a person falls overboard until safely recovered.

Under Sail

42. Hoist or unfurl sails correctly using halyards and/or furling devices. Describe the effect on sail trim or performance while adjusting each of the following lines and controls (if available on the training vessel): downhaul or cunningham, outhaul, boom vang, mainsheet, traveler, jibsheets, jibsheet fairleads. Discuss ways to reduce heeling.

43. Demonstrate correct winch operation including safety considerations for line tension/breakage, hand/finger position, winch handle insertion/removal, and clearing overrides.

Without coaching or assistance, verbalize appropriate commands and demonstrate competence, safety, and good seamanship in the role of Skipper/Helmsman during the maneuvers listed below. Honor all aids to navigation and use properly the Navigation Rules. Ensure sails are trimmed correctly and the vessel is in control at all times. Adjust sail controls appropriately as the vessel's heading changes and wind/sea conditions evolve.

BASIC COASTAL CRUISING STANDARD

44. Get out of 'irons' then select and maintain a given tack and course.

45. Head Up, Tack, Bear Away, and Jibe while pausing briefly at each of the following points of sail: Close Hauled, Close Reach, Beam Reach, Broad Reach, and Run (with sails "wing on wing").

46. Heave-to and then get sailing normally again.

47. While underway, reduce sail area by reefing mainsail and genoa; then shake out reef.

48. As crew, give appropriate verbal responses and perform correct actions during the maneuvers listed in #44 thru #47.

49. Describe and demonstrate the correct actions to be taken while *under sail* from the time a person falls overboard until safely recovered.

50. Lower and/or furl all sails and coil or flake and stow all lines properly.

Return to Dock/Slip

51. Ensure vessel/crew readiness and use the auxiliary engine to bring the vessel smoothly and under control to a stop next to a parallel dock or into a slip; secure the vessel using appropriate lines and fenders.

Knots

52. Describe the purpose of, and construct without assistance and in a timely manner, each of the following knots:
    - Figure-8
    - Clove Hitch
    - Cleat Hitch
    - Sheet Bend
    - Square (Reef) Knot
    - Round turn and 2 Half hitches
    - Bowline

Bareboat Cruising Standard (ASA 104)

PREREQUISITES: Basic Coastal Cruising (ASA 103) Certification, and the ability to demonstrate competencies in all knowledge and skills elements of those Standards. ASA recommends a minimum of 80 on-water sailing hours before undertaking ASA 104.

DESCRIPTION: Able to skipper a sloop-rigged, auxiliary powered keelboat of approximately 30 to 45 feet in length during a multi-day cruise upon inland or coastal waters in moderate to heavy winds (up to 30 knots) and sea conditions. Knowledge of provisioning, galley operations, boat systems, auxiliary engine operation, routine maintenance procedures, advanced sail trim, coastal navigation including basic chart plotting and GPS operation, multiple-anchor mooring, docking, health and safety, emergency operations, weather interpretation, and dinghy/tender operation.

KNOWLEDGE

Cruise Planning

1. Describe appropriate clothing and personal gear to pack for safety and comfort during a one-week cruise.

2. Describe the required documents and procedures for customs and immigration when cruising to a foreign port of entry.

3. Plan a menu and create a provisioning list for a one-week cruise.

4. Describe the symptoms and first aid treatments for hypothermia and heat exhaustion/heat stroke.

5. Describe the causes, prevention, and treatments for seasickness.

6. Describe the tools and spare parts that should be on board for a one-week cruise.

7. Describe variables that affect fuel consumption and cruising range under power, and calculate range based on average fuel consumption.

BAREBOAT CRUISING STANDARD

8. Describe the minimum daily water requirements for all personnel on board as well as methods to conserve fresh water.

Systems

9. Describe safe galley procedures to minimize dangers such as fire, scalding, and spillage.

10. Describe proper marine toilet operation, including precautions to prevent malfunction, and describe proper holding tank pump-out procedures.

11. Identify and describe the function of the fundamental systems and components of a marine diesel engine, including fuel, lubrication, cooling, and drive train.

12. Describe safe fresh water tank filling procedures, including identification of correct deck fills.

13. Describe power conservation measures and procedures to prevent battery depletion when anchored/moored overnight.

Emergencies

14. Name four acceptable distress signals, per the *USCG Navigation Rules and Regulations Handbook*, which are appropriate for a recreational vessel.

15. Describe actions to be taken in the following situations:
    - Collision with another boat
    - Running aground
    - Dragging Anchor
    - Flooding
    - Fire

16. Describe actions to be taken in the following situations when the vessel is under power:
    - Fouled Propeller
    - Engine cooling water fails to flow
    - Engine fails in a crowded anchorage where using sails is not possible
    - Engine fails in a busy channel

Seamanship

17. Describe the information required and the procedure for tying a boat to a fixed dock in areas with a large tidal range.

18. Describe the following multiple-anchor mooring procedures and their purposes:
    - Fore and Aft Moor
    - Forked Moor
    - Bahamian Moor
    - Mediterranean Moor

19. Describe methods and potential dangers of rafting vessels at anchor.

20. Describe safe methods for towing and securing a dinghy/tender.

21. Describe preparation of the vessel for heavy weather sailing including gear stowage, crew safety, and appropriate sail plan.

22. Describe the following courtesies and customs:
    - Permission to board
    - Permission to come alongside
    - Courtesy in crossing adjacent boats when rafted
    - Rights of first boat in an anchorage
    - Keeping clear of regattas
    - Flag etiquette
    - Rendering assistance to vessels in distress

23. Describe, using diagrams as appropriate, the applicable rules (steering & sailing, lights, and sound signals) for a 30' to 45' recreational vessel, as found in the *USCG Navigation Rules and Regulations Handbook*.

Navigation and Weather

24. Explain and identify the following coastal navigation terms using a chart or diagrams as appropriate:
    - Speed
    - Time
    - Distance
    - Tidal Range
    - Tidal Current
    - Track
    - Course
    - Heading
    - Bearing
    - Fix
    - True
    - Magnetic
    - Variation
    - Deviation
    - Line of Position (LOP)

BAREBOAT CRUISING STANDARD

25. Describe the sea breeze and land breeze dynamics and their effect on sailing conditions.

26. Identify conditions that may lead to the formation of radiation and sea/advection fog.

27. Describe actions to be taken in the following weather situations:
    - Fog/reduced visibility
    - Squall/thunderstorm

SKILLS

General

28. Perform the duties of skipper and crew on a live-aboard coastal cruise of at least 48 hours.

29. Locate and check the condition of all federally required equipment.

Systems

30. Perform a routine vessel inspection, ensuring that all systems and equipment are in working order, including:
    - Fuel level
    - Fresh water level
    - Battery voltage
    - Electrical system
    - Navigation lights
    - Instruments and electronics
    - Bilge
    - Through-hulls and seacocks
    - Standing rigging
    - Running rigging
    - Deck hardware
    - Ground tackle

31. Visually inspect the auxiliary engine. Check for correct engine oil level and potential problems such as leaking fluids or frayed belts; demonstrate safe engine starting, operating and stopping procedures.

32. Inspect the raw water strainer for debris and ensure that the raw water intake seacock is in the proper position for engine operation.

33. Locate the emergency steering tiller and identify where it attaches to the rudder post.

34. Operate the electric and manual bilge pumps to ensure they are functional.

35. Demonstrate proper operation of the VHF radio including hailing another station on Channel 16 and switching to a working channel.

36. Demonstrate proper operation of the galley stove including fuel supply, lighting, and shutting down; simulate the proper way to extinguish a galley fire.

37. Demonstrate the proper method of disconnecting and reconnecting shore power cables.

Under Power

38. Demonstrate the use of spring lines in the docking/undocking process (e.g., pivoting the vessel away from the dock during departure).

39. Maneuver the vessel in reverse gear, observing and explaining the effect of prop walk on the stern's direction.

40. Maneuver the boat in a confined space to include performing a 'standing turn' maneuver, turning the vessel 180 degrees using rudder position and gearshift/throttle control.

41. Ensure vessel/crew readiness and use the auxiliary engine to bring the vessel smoothly and under control to a stop next to a parallel dock or into a slip; secure the vessel using appropriate lines and fenders.

42. Describe/demonstrate an appropriate person in water (a.k.a. Man Overboard or MOB) recovery maneuver while *under power* and describe methods to bring the MOB safely back aboard.

43. Demonstrate one of the following multiple-anchor mooring methods as appropriate to local conditions using correct procedures such as hand signals, safety in handling ground tackle, proper operation of windlass (if equipped) and use of a snubber or bridle. Raise anchors and get underway smoothly using correct procedures.
    - Fore and Aft Moor
    - Forked Moor
    - Bahamian Moor
    - Mediterranean Moor

Under Sail

44. Sail a steady compass course within +/- 10 degrees, with sails trimmed properly.

45. Demonstrate the proper use of all available lines and sail controls (halyards, sheets, traveler, boom vang, outhaul, downhaul/cunningham, jibsheet fairleads, etc.) to obtain maximum performance and comfort.

46. Demonstrate the correct usage of a jibe preventer.

47. Demonstrate proper and appropriate reefing procedures while under sail or hove-to.

48. Demonstrate two different MOB recovery maneuvers while *under sail*; starting from both close-hauled and a broad reach and selecting an appropriate maneuver for each initial point of sail.

Navigation and Weather

49. Plan a coastal passage from origin to destination, plotting courses, distances, and waypoints. While en route, keep a written log, plot DR positions on a chart, and calculate estimated times of arrival (ETA) to waypoints.

50. Obtain and interpret marine weather information; describe the impact that the present observations and forecast may have on cruising plans over a 3-day period.

51. Obtain updated weather forecasts during a passage and compare with visual and measured observations.

52. Take visual 2- and 3-bearing fixes using a hand-bearing compass.

53. Determine the predicted depth above or below chart datum at a given time using tide prediction tables.

54. Use a GPS / chartplotter (if available) to obtain information and perform basic navigation functions such as position, course, speed, waypoints, ETA, and tidal information.

55. Pilot a boat into an unfamiliar harbor or anchorage by day using relevant nautical charts, publications, and tidal information.

Knots

56. Describe the purpose of and construct each of the following knots (without assistance and in a timely manner):
    - Figure-8
    - Square (Reef) knot
    - Clove hitch
    - Round turn and 2 half hitches
    - Cleat hitch
    - Bowline
    - Sheet bend
    - Rolling hitch
    - Trucker's hitch

Coastal Navigation Standard (ASA 105)

PREREQUISITES: None

DESCRIPTION: Able to apply the navigational theory and practices for safe navigation of a sailing vessel in coastal and inland waters. On-water coastal navigation skills elements are contained in the Basic Coastal Cruising, Bareboat Cruising, and Advanced Coastal Cruising Standards, in progressively increasing levels of detail.

KNOWLEDGE

1. Explain the chart symbols and conventions on U.S. nautical charts in accordance with the terminology of Chart #1.

2. Identify a source of official U.S. Coast Guard navigation publications.

3. Describe the publications required for prudent navigation in a local area including:
   - Large scale charts and Chart #1
   - Federal Requirements for Recreational Boats
   - *USCG Navigation Rules and Regulations Handbook*
   - State small vessel regulations
   - Local rules and regulations, if applicable
   - Local cruising guides
   - Tide and current tables (paper or electronic)
   - List of lights, buoys, and fog signals

4. Describe the instruments required for prudent navigation in a local area including:
   - Steering compass and deviation table
   - Handbearing compass and/or pelorus
   - Binoculars
   - Protractor or parallel rule
   - Depth sounder or leadline
   - Pencil, eraser, and notebook
   - Dividers
   - Chronometer
   - Log/knotmeter

5. Describe the purpose and example contents of a "Notice to Mariners."

6. Explain the terms and characteristics used for lighted navigation aids.

7. Explain the significance of shapes, colors, and lights used in the U.S. Aids to Navigation (ATON) system.

SKILLS

8. Use the tide and current tables to find:
   - Times and heights of tides at reference and secondary ports.
   - Direction and rate of current at referenced and secondary stations.

9. Convert courses and bearings between true, magnetic, and compass.

10. Check compass deviation by a transit bearing or other means.

11. Plot a dead reckoning position on a chart using speed, time and course to steer.

12. Allow for the effect of current and leeway to plot an estimated position.

13. Determine a course to steer which takes into account known current and leeway.

14. Determine current given course steered, speed, and two observed positions.

15. Plot a chart position from terrestrial objects using:
   - Two or more bearings on different objects taken simultaneously.
   - Bearings at different times (e.g., a running fix).
   - One bearing and a transit range.
   - One distance (e.g., a sounding or dipping a light) and one bearing.

16. Chart a course of at least 20 miles and three course changes using the above skills.

Advanced Coastal Cruising Standard (ASA 106)

PREREQUISITES: Bareboat Cruising (ASA 104) and Coastal Navigation (ASA 105) Certifications, and the ability to demonstrate all knowledge and skills elements of those Standards.

DESCRIPTION: Able to skipper and navigate a sailing vessel of approximately 30 to 50 feet in length in coastal and inland waters, in any conditions, day or night. Knowledge of sail theory and steering forces, advanced sail control, weather prediction using clouds and instruments, boat systems maintenance, heavy weather precautions, safety and seamanship.

KNOWLEDGE

1. Describe true and apparent wind.

2. Describe sailing forces using diagrams. Graphically find the center of effort and center of resistance of sails and keel, respectively.

3. Describe with the aid of diagrams the causes of lee and weather helm and methods of correcting them. Include reasons for preference of slight weather helm, sail selection (including full sails or reefed sails), mast position and mast rake.

4. Describe sail shapes and sail interactions as needed for different wind strengths and points of sail. Describe the effects on sail shape and sail interactions when adjusting the following:
   - Luff tension
   - Outhaul
   - Leech line
   - Boom vang
   - Backstay tension
   - Jib fairleads
   - Jib sheet tension
   - Mainsheet
   - Traveler
   - Downhaul/cunningham

ADVANCED COASTAL CRUISING STANDARD

Weather

5. Describe how to use a barometer and a thermometer independently and concurrently to assist in predicting weather.

6. Describe cirrus, cirrostratus, altocumulus, stratocumulus, cumulonimbus and cumulus clouds and the weather expected to be associated with each.

7. Describe local weather in relation to thermal winds and prevailing winds.

8. Describe three sources of marine weather information available in the United States.

Seamanship

9. Describe the proper selection of sails on a given boat for all weather conditions and give reasons for the selection made.

10. Describe appropriate heavy weather precautions and describe how they are carried out, including:
    - Sail changes
    - Use of special equipment such as safety harness and sea anchor
    - Doubling up of gear
    - Special checks in areas liable to chafe
    - Stowage of equipment above and below decks
    - Additional checks on bilge condition
    - Special arrangements for towing dinghy/tender
    - Problems of fatigue
    - Selection of clothing
    - The need of at least two on deck at all times.

11. Describe the steps to be taken by skipper and crew for "heaving to" and "lying a-hull."

12. Describe methods for rafting at anchor and possible risks with day and night rafting.

13. Describe how to prevent the dinghy/tender from riding up and bumping the vessel's hull while anchored at night.

14. Describe procedures for securing a boat overnight with one anchor and stern made fast to a dock or shoreline.

ADVANCED COASTAL CRUISING STANDARD

15. Describe two methods of using a second anchor to reduce swinging.

16. Describe four different methods of recovering a fouled anchor.

17. Describe when and how to use a trip line and an anchor buoy.

18. Describe when and how to set an anchor watch and the responsibilities of the crew on watch.

19. Describe how to:
    - Prepare a towing bridle
    - Pass a tow to another boat
    - Get underway with a tow using appropriate boat speed
    - Avoid fouling the propeller
    - Avoid danger of towline parting under stress
    - Make proper lookout arrangements during towing

20. List 8 of the 16 International Distress Signals found in Rule 37 of the *USCG Navigation Rules and Regulations Handbook*.

21. Describe how the boat should be handled and what actions should be taken when the following emergencies occur while under sail:
    - The boat is dismasted
    - The boat runs aground on a lee shore

22. Describe how the boat should be handled and what remedial action should be taken when the following emergencies occur while under power:
    - The engine cooling water fails to flow
    - The engine fails in a crowded anchorage
    - The engine fails in a busy channel

23. State the fuel tank capacity and range of a typical 40-foot cruising sailboat and the factors that could affect its range.

24. State the water tank capacity of a typical 40-foot cruising sailboat and the minimum water requirement per person.

ADVANCED COASTAL CRUISING STANDARD

25. Describe the skipper's responsibilities and action for the following common courtesies and customs:
    - Permission to board
    - Permission and entitlement to come alongside
    - Permission and entitlement to cross adjacent boats when rafted
    - Rights of first boat at an anchorage
    - Keep clear of boats racing
    - Flag etiquette: National flag, Courtesy flag, Burgee/house flag, Dipping flag
    - Checking of boat's appearance (shipshape and Bristol fashion, no lines or fenders dangling over side)
    - Duty to provide assistance at sea

26. List the documents required and describe the procedures followed when leaving and entering U.S. territorial waters.

Engineering

27. Describe appropriate measures for the following common engine problems:
    - Stoppage in fuel line
    - Burned and defective points
    - Fouled spark plug/injector problems
    - Carburetor icing (spring and fall sailing)
    - Unserviceable starter
    - Electrolysis

28. Describe when and how to carry out an engine oil change.

29. Describe minimum pre-season inspection and maintenance for the following:
    - Hull (including underwater fittings, electrical systems, painting, antifouling)
    - Spars and rigging (including electrolysis)
    - Sails
    - Safety

30. Describe recommended permanent and temporary installation methods of grounding for lightning.

31. List factors to be considered before allowing anyone to go swimming while the boat is at anchor.

32. Describe the danger of overhead power lines.

ADVANCED COASTAL CRUISING STANDARD

33. Describe the uses, capabilities and limitations of a portable radar reflector.

SKILLS

Boat Handling Under Sail

34. Perform the duties of skipper and crew on a liveaboard coastal cruise of at least 48 hours, including night sailing.

35. As helmsman, demonstrate the proper techniques of beating, reaching, running, tacking, jibing, heading up, bearing away, and luffing in approximately 20 knots of wind.

36. Work to weather to best advantage accounting for wind shifts, tides, current and local geography.

37. Sail a compass course within +/- 10 degrees with sails trimmed.

38. Demonstrate correct methods of towing a dinghy.

39. Demonstrate a person in water (Man Overboard or MOB) recovery maneuver while sailing at night.

40. Anchor, weigh anchor, pick up and cast off moorings while acting as helmsman and/or crew.

41. Demonstrate how to take a sounding using two different methods.

42. Stand a navigation watch during a passage of at least 20 miles by night and 20 miles by day and demonstrate all of the skills elements in the ASA Coastal Navigation Standard (105).

43. (Optional) Demonstrate correct procedures for hoisting, setting, trimming, jibing, dousing and packing a spinnaker.

Celestial Navigation Standard (ASA 107)

PREREQUISITE: None

DESCRIPTION: Able to apply celestial navigation theory and practices for safe navigation of a sailing vessel in offshore waters. On-water celestial navigation skills elements are demonstrated in the Offshore Passagemaking Standard (108).

1. Convert among standard time, zone time, and GMT/UTC.
2. Convert longitude into standard time, zone time, GMT/UTC.
3. Calculate the chronometer (or watch) error given a previous error and the daily rate.
4. Apply the corrections for index error, dip of the horizon, and total correction to convert sextant altitudes of the sun, stars, planets, and moon to true altitudes.
5. Calculate the time of meridian passage of the sun and calculate the boat's latitude from the observed meridian altitude of the sun.
6. Determine the latitude at twilight using Polaris.
7. Solve the navigational triangle using a navigation table and show all appropriate work.
8. Plot celestial lines of position on a Mercator projection or on a universal plotting sheet.
9. Calculate ship time and GMT/UTC of sunrise, sunset, and twilight.
10. Determine the approximate azimuths and altitudes of the navigational stars and planets at twilight.
11. Calculate and plot the lines of position obtained from observations of several celestial bodies at twilight and thus find the boat's position.
12. Advance the LOP obtained from a sun sight to another LOP obtained from the sun at a later time and find the boat's position using a running fix (Sun-run-Sun).
13. Calculate the true bearing of a low altitude celestial body in order to determine the error and deviation of the compass.

Offshore Passagemaking Standard (ASA 108)

PREREQUISITES: Coastal Navigation (ASA 105), Advanced Coastal Cruising (ASA 106) Certifications, and either the Celestial Navigation (ASA 107) Certification or the Basic Celestial Navigation (ASA 117) Endorsement, and the ability to demonstrate all knowledge and skills elements of those Standards.

DESCRIPTION: Able to skipper a sailing vessel on extended offshore passages requiring celestial navigation. Knowledge of long-term passage planning, offshore vessel selection, sail repair, offshore first aid, watch-keeping, emergency procedures, abandon ship protocols, safety and seamanship.

KNOWLEDGE

Passage Planning

1. Plan a passage across the North Atlantic or Pacific and state the advantages, disadvantages and hazards of various routes, utilizing Ocean Passages for the World, climatic charts, Great Circle plotting charts, plotting instruments, etc.

2. Plot a series of rhumb lines on a Mercator chart to approximate a great circle route.

3. Describe the publications required for prudent navigation on an offshore passage including:
   - Coastal charts and publications
   - Work sheets
   - Ocean Passages for the World
   - Nautical almanac
   - Sight reduction tables
   - Plotting sheets
   - Voyage Preparation

4. Describe the effect of the following factors when selecting a offshore ocean passage of at least 1000 miles:
   - Hull Shape
   - Rudder
   - Machinery
   - Sails
   - Hull construction
   - Keel
   - Water capacity
   - Interior Layout
   - Displacement
   - Rig
   - Fuel Capacity

5. List essential items for minor repairs to vessel, rigging and sails.

6. Describe various items required to prevent chafe.

7. Describe the advantages and disadvantages of three different self-steering methods/devices.

8. Plan meals for a minimum of four people on a seven day offshore passage.

9. Describe proper methods for preserving/storing food and the expected storage life of different types of food.

10. Describe the following factors to be considered when selecting crew members for an offshore passage:
    - Health
    - Attitude
    - Compatibility
    - Experience
    - Physical capability

12. Describe suitable clothing for an offshore voyage.

13. State a source of obtaining advanced first aid information while on an offshore passage.

14. Identify and describe the basic treatment of potential medical problems.

15. Describe methods of preventing injury to the cook or nearby persons while cooking at sea.

16. List items carried in an offshore first aid kit.

17. Prepare and file a float plan.

Shipboard Routines

18. Describe three watch-keeping systems and the advantages and disadvantages of each.

19. Describe alternate watch-keeping arrangements in the event crew members are incapacitated.

20. Describe the duties of the on-watch and off-watch crew.

21. Establish a routine maintenance schedule to periodically check the following items:
    - Bilges
    - Sea cocks
    - Rigging
    - Hatches
    - Helm
    - Galley and supplies
    - Fuel and water
    - Machinery
    - Safety equipment
    - Electronic equipment

22. Set up a routine vessel cleaning schedule.

Emergency Procedures

23. Describe how to rig a trailing Man Overboard (MOB) line with an alarm.

24. Describe an alternative method of alerting the crew to a MOB situation. State other emergency situations when you should limit the use of this device.

25. Describe what actions should be taken when a MOB is not located on the first pass.

26. Describe how to organize the crew for a routine fire drill.

27. Describe possible methods of jury rigging a vessel in the event of dismasting and what course should then be assumed.

28. Describe proper actions to be taken after a vessel has been struck by lightning.

29. List essential survival items to be kept in a standby kit in the event the vessel must be abandoned offshore.

30. Describe additional useful survival and rescue items.

31. State the dangers that might be encountered in a small life raft at sea.

32. List safety equipment that should be carried in addition to Federally required items.

Navigation Rules

33. Describe, using diagrams as appropriate, the applicable rules for an offshore sailing vessel, as found in the *USCG Navigation Rules and Regulations Handbook*.

34. List the 16 International Distress Signals found in Rule 37 of the *USCG Navigation Rules and Regulations Handbook*.

SKILLS

35. Act as skipper and crew on an offshore passage of no less than 600nm and 72 hours, a part of which is at least 251nm offshore.

36. Obtain a celestial fix using a Sun-Run-Sun or three (3) celestial bodies.

37. Obtain a celestial heading check.

38. Apply all elements of the ASA Celestial Navigation Standard (ASA 107) or the ASA Basic Celestial Navigation Endorsement (ASA 117).

Basic Small Boat Sailing Standard (ASA 110)

PREREQUISITES: None

DESCRIPTION: Able to skipper a non-ballasted centerboard/daggerboard monohull or multihull sailboat of approximately 8 to 20 feet in length by day in light to moderate winds (up to 15 knots) and sea conditions. Knowledge of basic sailing terminology, sail trim, points of sail, crew responsibilities, seamanship and safety including capsize avoidance/recovery and navigation rules to avoid collisions.

NOTE: Items marked with an asterisk (*) apply to multihulls only.

KNOWLEDGE

1. Identify and describe the following sailboat parts and their functions:
   - Hull
   - Foredeck
   - Transom
   - Centerboard
   - Centerboard trunk
   - Daggerboard
   - Mast
   - Mast step
   - Boom
   - Gooseneck
   - Bow
   - Stern
   - Tiller
   - Rudder
   - Pintle
   - Gudgeon
   - Shroud
   - Spreader
   - Forestay
   - Cam cleat
   - T-cleat
   - Block
   - Jib fairlead
   - Cockpit
   - Hiking strap
   - Clevis pin
   - Cotter pin/ring
   - Trampoline*
   - Righting line*
   - Tiller cross bar*

2. Identify and describe the functions of the following sails, sail parts, and sail controls:
   - Mainsail
   - Jib
   - Tack
   - Head
   - Clew
   - Luff
   - Foot
   - Leech
   - Bolt rope
   - Halyard
   - Mainsheet
   - Jib sheet
   - Boom vang
   - Outhaul
   - Traveler
   - Hank
   - Telltale
   - Shackle
   - Batten
   - Batten pocket
   - Downhaul/cunningham

BASIC SMALL BOAT SAILING STANDARD

3. Define the following locational, directional, relative, and other terms:
   - Port
   - Aft
   - Astern
   - Leeward
   - Turtle
   - Starboard
   - Heel
   - Abeam
   - Sculling
   - Fly a hull *
   - Forward
   - Ahead
   - Windward
   - Capsize

Wind Awareness, Boat Control, and Points of Sail

4. Describe visual and non-visual indicators that may be used to provide a sense of wind direction and strength.

5. Describe the force generated as air flows over a sail when sailing upwind, and how a sail works differently when sailing downwind.

6. Describe how to adjust steering and sails as wind speed and direction change relative to the boat.

7. Describe proper adjustments to the centerboard/daggerboard, sails, and crew positions before and during the following maneuvers:
   - Heading up
   - Bearing away
   - Tacking
   - Jibing

8. Describe methods of accelerating, decelerating, and stopping a sailboat.

9. Describe and identify the following points of sail and sailboat positions relative to the wind:
   - No sail zone
   - Port tack
   - Close reach
   - Run
   - In irons
   - Starboard tack
   - Beam reach
   - Sailing by the lee
   - Head to wind
   - Close hauled
   - Broad reach

10. Describe how the sails, crew and centerboard/daggerboard should be positioned for each point of sail.

BASIC SMALL BOAT SAILING STANDARD

Seamanship

11. List all federally required equipment and examples of recommended equipment to be carried aboard a sailboat of less than 20 feet.

12. List the tasks that must be accomplished when setting up or rigging a small sailboat.

13. Describe the types of personal gear that is appropriate to bring on a small sailboat and the benefits and methods of stowing and securing gear and equipment properly.

14. List sources of information concerning local sailing conditions including weather, tides, currents, wind, fog, storms, and other hazards.

15. Describe, using diagrams as appropriate, the applicable rules for a 20-foot recreational sailing vessel, as found in the *USCG Navigation Rules and Regulations Handbook*.

16. Describe the risks of departing from and returning to a beach with waves, and methods to avoid damage and injury.

17. Describe the causes and risks associated with an accidental jibe and ways in which it can be prevented.

18. Describe methods for getting a sailboat out of irons and under control onto a desired tack.

19. Describe the risks associated with cold or hot weather and water temperature, what is appropriate clothing for different conditions, and how to prevent temperature-related ailments.

20. Describe the risks associated with overhead power lines as related to trailering, launching and sailing.

21. Describe why it is critical to wear lifejackets and know the location and correct operation of all safety equipment.

22. State different ways a sailboat can capsize and describe how to prevent and recover from a capsize.

23. Describe how to prevent running aground and recovery procedures from a grounding.

BASIC SMALL BOAT SAILING STANDARD

24. Describe means for prevention, and procedures for recovering a person in the water (Man Overboard, or MOB), including how to maneuver the sailboat safely back to the person.

25. Describe an internationally recognized distress signal that can be made while on board a sailboat or in the water.

SKILLS

Readiness and Getting Underway

26. Select clothing appropriate for the expected sailing conditions.

27. Put on a life jacket, ensuring it is serviceable and fits properly.

28. Perform a pre-departure inspection to verify the sailboat is safe and ready for sailing, including a check of safety equipment and proper stowage of gear on board.

29. Set up mast and rigging (as applicable); attach and ready all sails, boat parts and lines properly.

30. Launch the sailboat into the water using available equipment (e.g., trailer, hoist or dolly), as applicable.

31. Board the sailboat, safely distributing persons while maintaining stability.

32. Secure and properly position the rudder and centerboard/daggerboard, as applicable.

33. Orient for departure by determining and pointing to the wind direction (and oncoming waves if beach launching).

34. Raise sail(s) using appropriate sequence.

35. Get underway by pushing or turning the sailboat in appropriate direction and utilizing proper steering, crew position, and sail trim.

BASIC SMALL BOAT SAILING STANDARD

Maneuvering the Sailboat

36. Use proper steering and sail trim to keep the sailboat under control.

37. Avoid potential collisions by observing the Navigation Rules.

38. Ensure the main halyard is properly tensioned, then adjust the boom vang, downhaul/cunningham and outhaul, if available, while sailing on a close reach.

39. Use sail trim to decrease and increase the speed of the sailboat.

40. Hold a steady course using proper steering, crew position and sail trim.

41. Bear away from a close reach to a broad reach using proper steering, crew position and sail trim.

42. Head up from a broad reach to a close reach using proper steering, crew position and sail trim.

43. Stop the sailboat completely while sailing on a close reach.

44. Accelerate and resume sailing on a close reach after having been stopped.

45. Place the sailboat in irons and then get out of irons using appropriate techniques.

46. Bear away from a broad reach to a run, avoiding an unintentional jibe by identifying and listing indicators that a jibe is imminent.

47. Tack the boat from close-hauled to close-hauled avoiding getting stuck in irons and using proper steering, crew position, sail trim and verbal commands (if crew on board).

48. Jibe the boat from broad reach to broad reach keeping the sailboat in control and using proper steering, crew position, sail trim and verbal commands (if crew on board).

Towing and Recovery Procedures

49. Accept and secure a bow tow and/or side tow and maneuver safely, if a towing boat is available.

50. Demonstrate the correct actions to be taken while under sail from the time a person falls overboard until safely recovered.

51. Return a capsized sailboat (if boat in use is able to be capsized with relative ease) to an upright position and re-enter the boat, using appropriate techniques.

52. Use a righting line to return a capsized multihull to an upright position.*

Returning to Shore

53. Plan a safe arrival at shore (slip, dock, mooring, beach), bring the boat to a stop at the desired location, and lower sails using appropriate techniques..

54. Get off the boat safely while maintaining stability.

55. Retrieve the sailboat from the water using available equipment (e.g., trailer, hoist or dolly), as applicable.

56. Stow all lines, sails and gear, including properly furling, flaking, or folding all sails.

Line Handling and Knots

57. Demonstrate techniques for coiling and flaking lines.

58. Throw a line accurately toward an intended target and receive a thrown line from another individual.

59. Describe the purpose of, and construct in a timely manner, each of the following knots and hitches:
    - Figure-8 Knot
    - Square (Reef) Knot
    - Clove Hitch
    - Bowline
    - Cleat Hitch
    - Round Turn & 2 Half Hitches

Sailing Review (ASA 111)

PREREQUISITES: Basic Keelboat Sailing (ASA 101) Certification

DESCRIPTION: Desire to improve or re-familiarize sailing knowledge and skills imparted during previous on-the-water ASA certification course(s). Student and Instructor jointly decide on goals prior to the start of the review. Instructor provides student with a written, personalized Recommended Plan and Logbook remarks suggesting steps for continued improvement in knowledge and skills proficiencies after the review is completed. This review may be taken multiple times.

KNOWLEDGE

At the Dock

1. Review of Knowledge elements, as applicable, of ASA 101, 103, 104, 106, 114 Certification Standards by an ASA Instructor with the appropriate corresponding ASA Instructor Certification(s).

SKILLS

Underway

2. Review of Skills elements, as applicable, of ASA 101, 103, 104, 106, 114 Certification Standards by an ASA Instructor with the appropriate corresponding ASA Instructor Certification(s).

Cruising Catamaran Standard (ASA 114)

PREREQUISITES: Bareboat Cruising (ASA 104) Certification, and the ability to demonstrate competency in all knowledge and skills elements of those Standards.

DESCRIPTION: Able to skipper an auxiliary-powered sailing cruising catamaran of approximately 30 to 45 feet in length during a multi-day liveaboard cruise upon inland or coastal waters in moderate to heavy winds (up to 30 knots) and sea conditions. Knowledge of catamaran structure, components and features, performance under sail and power, boat systems, seamanship and safety, heavy weather operation, and emergency response.

KNOWLEDGE

Catamaran Terminology

1. Identify and describe the functions of the following terms and structural components:
   - Catamaran
   - Hull
   - Nacelle
   - Full Bridgedeck
   - Partial Bridgedeck
   - Deckhouse
   - Crossbeams
   - Fixed keel
   - Daggerboard
   - Escape hatch
   - Trampoline
   - Bridle
   - Twin engine
   - Mainsail roach
   - Dolphin Striker
   - Seagull Striker

2. Identify and describe the functions of the following rigging terms and components:
   - Fractional rig
   - Tripod rig
   - Diamond stays
   - Spreaders
   - Shrouds
   - Forestay

Catamaran Features and Performance

3. Describe the accommodations of a typical catamaran and their effect on comfort and safety.

4. Compare differences in operating and living aboard a monohull and catamaran of similar length.

5. Describe the impact that a catamaran's deck structures may have on visibility from the helm.

CRUISING CATAMARAN STANDARD

6. Describe stability differences between a ballasted monohull keelboat and a catamaran.

7. Describe load-carrying characteristics of a catamaran and how weight distribution affects safety and performance.

8. Describe shoal draft keels on a catamaran and the impact on cruise planning and sailing.

9. Describe the typical installation of daggerboards and how they affect performance.

10. Describe catamaran engine placement and the effect on performance and balance.

11. Describe maneuverability under power of a twin-engine catamaran.

12. Describe the effects of windage on close-quarters maneuverability under power

13. Describe the effects of windage on sailing performance.

14. List differences in sailing performance between a monohull and a catamaran of similar size.

15. Describe how to use the jib to counteract the weather-vane effect of a catamaran's mainsail when tacking.

16. List various sail combinations utilized on a catamaran and how they affect the center of effort.

17. List differences between the mainsails of a monohull keelboat and a catamaran.

18. Describe indicators for and conditions under which a catamaran's sails should be reefed.

Catamaran Systems

19. List differences in the types of boat systems typically installed on monohulls versus catamarans.

20. Describe freshwater and fuel storage tank placement and precautions on a catamaran.

21. Describe battery-charging options, including alternators, shore power and generator, and how they affect twin-engine catamarans.

Seamanship

22. Describe options for gear stowage and proper stowing procedures.

23. Describe the features of a catamaran galley and methods of working safely in the galley.

24. Compare options for hoisting, carrying and towing a dinghy.

25. Describe methods and limitations of rafting a catamaran with other boats.

26. Describe the use of a bridle with a single bow anchor or fixed mooring.

27. Describe the following multiple-anchor mooring procedures on a catamaran and the circumstances under which they could be used:
    - Fore & Aft Moor
    - Bahamian Moor
    - Mediterranean Moor

Heavy Weather Operation and Emergency Response

28. Describe conditions that may contribute to capsizing a catamaran and practices to avoid capsizing.

29. Describe post-capsize response procedures.

30. Describe where and how to attach jacklines and tethered safety harnesses on a catamaran.

31. Describe how the structure and performance of a catamaran under both sail and power affects the recovery of a person in the water (a.k.a. Man Overboard or MOB).

32. Describe heavy weather sailing practices applied to a catamaran, including:
    - Lying a-hull
    - Heaving-to
    - Downwind speed control

33. Describe actions to be taken if one or both engines fail.

34. Identify the emergency steering tiller and indicate where it attaches to the controlling rudder post.

CRUISING CATAMARAN STANDARD

SKILLS

Pre-Departure

35. Locate and check the condition of all required and ASA recommended equipment.
36. Perform a routine vessel inspection, ensuring that all systems and equipment are in working order.

Under Power

37. Depart safely from a dock when the approximate wind direction is (a) parallel to the dock and (b) perpendicular to the dock.
38. Demonstrate the proper use of spring lines to pivot the catamaran during dock departure and return.
39. Ensure vessel and crew readiness and use the auxiliary engines to bring the catamaran smoothly to a controlled stop next to a parallel dock or into a slip; then secure the vessel using appropriate lines and fenders.
40. Make way ahead and turn the catamaran in a tight circle, comparing the turning radius between three different engine gear selections:
    - Both engines in forward gear
    - One engine in forward, the other in neutral
    - One engine in forward, the other in reverse
41. Make way astern and turn the catamaran in a tight circle.
42. Steer a straight, controlled course astern for at least five boat lengths.
43. Approach a mark under power upwind, downwind, and with wind abeam, in each case stopping the catamaran within 10 feet of the mark.
44. Approach a mooring buoy (or suitable substitute if no mooring is available), attach to the mooring using a bridle, then cast off from the mooring and get underway.
45. Maneuver the catamaran under power in a confined space, compensating for wind and current effects.
46. Demonstrate the correct actions to be taken while under power to recover a MOB.

47. Demonstrate two of the following anchor/mooring methods as appropriate to local conditions, using correct procedures including hand signals, safety in handling ground tackle, proper operation of windlass and use of a bridle. Raise anchor(s) and get underway using correct procedures.
    - Single bow anchor
    - Fore and aft moor
    - Bahamian Moor
    - Mediterranean Moor

Under Sail

48. Sail a steady compass course, varying the heading no more than +/- 10 degrees, with sails trimmed properly.

49. Demonstrate proper usage of all lines and sail controls (halyards, sheets, traveler, boom vang, outhaul, downhaul, etc.) that are available on the catamaran to obtain maximum performance and comfort.

50. Demonstrate proper combined usage of the mainsheet and traveler for upwind and downwind sailing.

51. Demonstrate how to get out of "irons."

52. Perform each of the following maneuvers separately and under control, giving appropriate commands and ensuring proper sail trim:
    - Head Up
    - Bear Away
    - Tack
    - Jibe
    - Heave to

53. Hold a steady course on each of the following points of sail, ensuring proper sail trim:
    - Close Hauled
    - Close Reach
    - Beam Reach
    - Broad Reach

54. Luff sails while sailing on a close reach at maximum safe speed for the conditions, noting the length of time required for the catamaran to come to a stop. Re-trim sails and note the length of time required to accelerate to maximum safe speed.

55. Demonstrate the correct use of a jibe preventer.

CRUISING CATAMARAN STANDARD

56. Demonstrate proper reefing procedures while under sail or hove-to.
57. Demonstrate the proper actions to be taken while under sail to recover a MOB, using two different recovery methods.

Basic Celestial Navigation Endorsement (ASA 117)

PREREQUISITES: None

DESCRIPTION: Able to apply basic celestial navigation theory and practice to determine latitude and longitude at sea using a sextant and *Nautical Almanac*.

1. Describe the terms and theory of Basic Celestial Navigation.

Using a traditional sextant and Nautical Almanac and without the use of a programmed calculator or computer:

2. Convert among standard time, zone time, and GMT/UTC.
3. Convert longitude into standard time, zone time, GMT/UTC.
4. Determine the times of sunrise, sunset and civil twilight for a vessel's position.
5. Describe and identify the parts, principles and operation of a traditional sextant.
6. Determine altitudes of the Sun and Polaris by a traditional sextant.
7. Obtain Latitude and Longitude at noon (LAN) by applying the sextant corrections for conversions of the raw sextant altitudes (hs) of the Sun to the true celestial altitudes (HO) of the Sun.
8. Determine the vessel's latitude and Estimated Position at morning and evening twilight by means of the altitude of Polaris.
9. Plot latitudes and EPs on a chart.

Docking Endorsement (ASA 118)

PREREQUISITES: None.

DESCRIPTION: Able to safely and efficiently dock an auxiliary powered (single inboard or outboard engine) sailboat. Knowledge of basic auxiliary power theory, engine and steering controls, proper use of dock lines, crew communication and safety.

KNOWLEDGE

1. List four forces that act on a boat during docking maneuvers, how each force affects the speed and orientation of the boat, which force is dominant.
2. Describe which forces the helmsman can control or use to advantage during docking.
3. Describe engine and rudder control as used during docking.
4. Describe how to properly secure mooring lines in a slip and alongside a dock.
5. Describe the use of spring lines during docking.
6. Describe safety considerations during docking.
7. Describe docking and undocking procedures including crewmember duties.

SKILLS

8. Prepare boat and crewmembers for docking and undocking including:
   - Assessment of boat condition
   - Dock and fairway configuration
   - Routes of exit and entry
   - Water depths
   - Wind and current direction and strength
   - Potential hazards
   - Docking/undocking plan
   - Crewmember assignments and instruction
   - Emergency abort options and procedures

9. Maneuver the boat in a confined space to include performing a 'standing turn' maneuver, turning the vessel 360 degrees using rudder position and gearshift/throttle control while remaining in a circle not exceeding two boat lengths in diameter.

10. Undock boat as planned without collision, grounding, damage or injury.

11. Dock parallel to a dock with wind blowing towards dock; demonstrate proper use of spring lines and attachment of lines to the dock.

12. Undock from parallel to a dock with wind blowing towards dock; demonstrate proper use of spring lines to avoid other boats moored fore and aft.

13. Dock bow into slip with a cross wind; demonstrate proper use of spring lines and attachment of lines in the slip.

14. Dock stern into slip with a cross wind; demonstrate proper use of spring lines and attachment of lines in the slip.

15. Demonstrate the proper method for heaving a line.

16. Construct and demonstrate the use of each of the following:
    - Round turn and 2 Half hitches
    - Cleat Hitch
    - Bowline

Marine Weather Endorsement (ASA 119)

PREREQUISITES: None

DESCRIPTION: Able to observe and forecast weather conditions using traditional maritime skills and modern technology. Knowledge of weather information for planning and adapting navigation during short duration and extended voyages.

Basic Concepts

1. Describe the role of marine weather in boating plans, particularly wind forecasting.
2. Describe the relationship of temperature, precipitation, visibility, wind, and waves and their impact on forecasting.
3. Describe wind terminology and units used in speed, distances, temperatures and pressures.
4. Utilize data from the Ocean Prediction Center, National Data Buoy Center, and Marine Weather Service (NWS) Charts.

Pressure and Wind

5. Describe the relationship between pressure and wind, including the flow of wind around highs, lows, ridges and troughs.
6. Convert apparent wind to true wind.
7. Calibrate and take readings from aneroid and digital barometers.
8. Describe pressure distributions and related labeling practices on weather maps.
9. Predict wind speed and direction from isobars on a weather map.

Global Winds and Currents

10. Describe the basic properties of the atmosphere and its influence on wind and weather.
11. Describe basic air mass classifications and vertical stability.

12. Describe the role of equatorial heating in establishing the doldrums, horse latitudes, trade winds and prevailing westerlies.

13. Describe the role of the poles in generating low fronts, and how these subsequently cross the mid-latitudes of the globe.

14. Describe the origins and behavior of winds aloft and how they contribute to the development and transport of surface systems around the globe.

15. Describe the distribution of ocean currents around the globe and how to predict their values for the purpose of voyage planning.

Strong Wind Systems

16. Describe forecasting conventions and warnings available for strong wind systems.

17. List the distinctions between lows and fronts, and between tropical and extra-tropical storms.

18. Describe how to predict squall behavior.

19. Describe how to finding and use satellite wind measurements.

20. Describe typical behaviors of tropical depressions, storms, and hurricanes.

Clouds, Fog, and Sea State

21. Describe and identify 10 basic cloud types and what they might indicate.

22. Describe the sequence of clouds expected during a frontal passage.

23. Describe how fog forms and how it is forecasted.

24. Describe the practical distinctions between sea fog and radiation fog and between swells, wind waves and ripple.

25. Describe how to predict wave height and speed based on wind speed, duration, and fetch.

26. Describe the Beaufort Wind Force scale that relates wind speed to sea state.

Wind and Terrain

27. Describe how the presence and topography of land affects wind flow over adjacent waters.

28. Describe prominent local winds such as: sea breezes, land breezes, channeling & gap winds, blocking & lifting, and downslope winds.

29. Describe the interaction between thermal winds and pressure system winds.

Weather Maps

30. List types of weather maps available and how to access them at home and underway.

31. Describe the process of weather routing, including sequencing of analyses and forecasts to confirm forecasts.

32. Describe how to access and use GRIB forecasts, taking into account their pros and cons compared to analyzed products prepared by meteorologists.

33. Describe how to use 500-mb maps and weather discussions to help evaluate surface forecasts.

34. Describe how to use shipboard observations of wind and pressure to evaluate analyses and subsequent forecasts.

Sources of Weather Data

35. Compare the use of both traditional and modern sources of climatic data for planning the time and route of voyages — for inland and coastal voyaging, as well as ocean crossings.

36. List sources for weather data underway and wireless options for obtaining it.

37. Describe the distinctions and pros and cons of commercial weather services compared to free public services from the NWS.

38. Describe the role of professional weather routing services and how they might fit into voyaging plans.

On-board Forecasting and Tactics

39. Describe the proper use of barometer, wind speed, wind direction, clouds, and sea state for shipboard forecasting.
40. Describe how to gauge the direction of winds aloft from cirrus cloud patterns.
41. Give examples of maritime weather proverbs and which ones have value in forecasting.
42. Describe the role of weather routing in improving sailing tactics.

Southern Hemisphere Weather

43. Describe unique aspects of Southern Hemisphere weather.
44. List sources for weather information specific to the Southern Hemisphere.

Radar Endorsement (ASA 120)

PREREQUISITES: Coastal Navigation (ASA 105) Certification.

DESCRIPTION: Able to properly use small-craft radar (or radar simulator) for piloting, navigation, and collision avoidance. Knowledge of radar principles and practical matters of radar operation.

1. Describe the principles of radar and how it works, including:
   - Overview of system components
   - Microwave pulse and beam structure
   - Radar target characteristics
   - Range of detection, scanner design, and mounting options
   - Power requirements
   - Radiation safety near radar scanners

2. Demonstrate basic radar operation, including:
   - Power on, warm up, and initial adjustments
   - Gain adjustments
   - Use of anti-clutter controls for rain (FTC) and sea state (STC)
   - Pros and cons of optional display modes: Head-up, North-up, and Course-up
   - Optimizing pulse-length selection
   - Measuring target range and bearing with VRM, EBL, and cursor mode
   - Use of guard sectors and alarms
   - Optimizing radar picture for specific observations

3. Interpret the radar screen, including:
   - Radar shadows
   - Effect of horizontal beam width on target images
   - Effect of pulse length on target images
   - Identifying interference and other unwanted echoes

4. Demonstrate the use of radar for piloting a vessel, including:
   - Use of radar to hold a desired course
   - Use of electronic range and bearing line (ERBL)
   - Finding and keeping track of position relative to prominent landmarks
   - Identifying distant harbors or channels
   - Rounding a corner at a safe distance off the shore
   - Anchoring with radar

5. Demonstrate radar position navigation, including:
   - Coordinating electronic chart displays with the radar screen
   - Quick radar range and bearing confirmation of GPS positions
   - Accurate multi-range fixes using radar

6. Demonstrate how to use radar for assisting with collision avoidance, including:
   - Use and value of target trails and wakes
   - Tracking targets with EBL and VRM
   - Estimating time, range and bearing to closest point of approach (CPA)
   - Figuring true course and speed of approaching targets (relative motion diagram)
   - Determining expected running lights based on radar observations
   - Rules of thumb for radar maneuvering
   - Radar reflectors
   - Overview of ARPA and AIS

7. Describe and demonstrate the use of radar in conjunction with the *USCG Navigations Rules and Regulations Handbook* including:
   - Role of radar in evaluating collision risk
   - Cautions (limitations) for radar use
   - Requirements for checking various ranges and adjustments
   - Application of Rule 19 (d) — when detecting a converging target by radar alone

Online Achievements

PREREQUISITES: None

DESCRIPTION: This section is to log acknowledgement of completion for online courses offered by ASA . These online courses are not part of the ASA core curriculum, but should be viewed as supplemental education or extracurricular study.

Date / Course Name	
Date Course Name	**AFFIX SEAL HERE**
Date Course Name	**AFFIX SEAL HERE**
Date Course Name	**AFFIX SEAL HERE**
Date Course Name	**AFFIX SEAL HERE**

ONLINE ACHIEVEMENTS

Date	
Course Name	**AFFIX SEAL HERE**

Date	
Course Name	**AFFIX SEAL HERE**

Date	
Course Name	**AFFIX SEAL HERE**

Date	
Course Name	**AFFIX SEAL HERE**

Date	
Course Name	**AFFIX SEAL HERE**

Instructor Certification Requirements

Following are the prerequisites and requirements for Instructor Certification. Instructor Qualification Clinics (IQCs) are held throughout the United States and Internationally. Qualified individuals should consult the ASA Website for the current schedule of IQCs and registration information.

ASA 200 INSTRUCTOR PREPARATION

PREREQUISITES:
- Minimum 18, 20, or 25 years of age as per Certification
- A current Sailing Instructor credential
- Approval by the ASA IE Council

REQUIREMENTS:
- Successful completion of ASA 200 IQC

ASA 201 BASIC KEELBOAT SAILING INSTRUCTOR

PREREQUISITES:
- Minimum 18 years of age
- Minimum score of 90% on the ASA 101 Examination

REQUIREMENTS:
- Minimum score of 75% on the ASA 201 Examination
- Successful completion of the ASA 201 IQC

AUTHORIZED TO CERTIFY:
- ASA 101 Basic Keelboat Sailing
- ASA 111 Sailing Review for ASA 101 Elements

BASIC COASTAL CRUISING INSTRUCTOR (203)

PREREQUISITES:
- Basic Keelboat Sailing Instructor (201)

REQUIREMENTS:
- Successful completion of the Basic Coastal Cruising IQC

AUTHORIZED TO CERTIFY:
- Basic Coastal Cruising (103)
- Sailing Review (111) for ASA 103 elements

BAREBOAT CRUISING INSTRUCTOR (204)

PREREQUISITES:
- Basic Coastal Cruising Instructor (203)

REQUIREMENTS:
- Successful completion of the Bareboat Cruising IQC

AUTHORIZED TO CERTIFY:
- Bareboat Cruising (104)
- Sailing Review (111) for ASA 104 elements

COASTAL NAVIGATION INSTRUCTOR (205)

PREREQUISITES:
- Basic Coastal Cruising Instructor (203)

REQUIREMENTS:
- Successful completion of the Coastal Navigation IQC
- Minimum score of 90% on the Coastal Navigation Examination

AUTHORIZED TO CERTIFY:
- Coastal Navigation (105)

ASA 206 ADVANCED COASTAL CRUISING INSTRUCTOR

PREREQUISITES:
- Minimum 20 years of age
- ASA 204, ASA 205

REQUIREMENTS:
- Minimum score of 90% on the ASA 206 Examination
- Successful completion of the ASA 206 IQC

AUTHORIZED TO CERTIFY:
- ASA 106 Advanced Coastal Cruising
- ASA 111 Sailing Review for ASA 106 Elements

INSTRUCTOR CERTIFICATION REQUIREMENTS

CELESTIAL NAVIGATION INSTRUCTOR (207)

PREREQUISITES:
- Bareboat Cruising Instructor (204)
- Coastal Navigation Instructor (205)

REQUIREMENTS:
- Minimum score of 90% on the Celestial Navigation Examination

AUTHORIZED TO CERTIFY:
- Celestial Navigation (107)
- Basic Celestial Navigation Endorsement (117)

ASA 208 OFFSHORE PASSAGEMAKING INSTRUCTOR

PREREQUISITES:
- Minimum 25 years of age
- ASA 206, ASA 207 or ASA 217
- At least 300 teaching hours as an ASA 206 Instructor
- Skipper an offshore passage that:
    - is non-stop for at least 600nm and 72 hours
    - at some point reaches at least 251nm offshore
- Approval by the IE Council

REQUIREMENTS:
- Successful completion of the ASA 208 IQC

AUTHORIZED TO CERTIFY:
- ASA 108 Offshore Passagemaking

BASIC SMALL BOAT SAILING INSTRUCTOR (210)

PREREQUISITES:
- Minimum 18 years of age

REQUIREMENTS:
- Successful completion of the Basic Small Boat Sailing IQC

AUTHORIZED TO CERTIFY:
- Basic Small Boat Sailing (110)

CRUISING CATAMARAN INSTRUCTOR (214)

PREREQUISITES:
- Bareboat Cruising Instructor (204)

REQUIREMENTS:
- Successful completion of the Cruising Catamaran IQC

AUTHORIZED TO CERTIFY:
- Cruising Catamaran (114)
- Sailing Review (111) for ASA 114 elements

Instructor Certifications

Instructors who acquire the following Certification Seals are then authorized to teach the corresponding Student Certifications. See also Student Certification Seals on pages 13-16, Student Certification Standards on pages 19-61, and Instructor Certification Standards on pages 73-76.

THIS IS TO CERTIFY THAT:

_____
Name

has successfully achieved the following ASA Instructor Standards:

200 **ASA Instructor Preparation**	AFFIX SEAL HERE Provisional Certification for three (3) months until seal is affixed

Date

ASA Instructor · Instructor Number

ASA Certification Facility · Aboard (Type/Design of Sailboat)

201 **Basic Keelboat Sailing Instructor**	AFFIX SEAL HERE Provisional Certification for three (3) months until seal is affixed

Date

ASA Instructor · Instructor Number

ASA Certification Facility · Aboard (Type/Design of Sailboat)

INSTRUCTOR CERTIFICATIONS

THIS IS TO CERTIFY THAT:

_____
Name

has successfully achieved the following ASA Instructor Standards:

203
Basic Coastal Cruising Instructor

AFFIX SEAL HERE

Provisional Certification
for three (3) months
until seal is affixed

_____
Date

_____
ASA Instructor   Instructor Number

_____
ASA Certification Facility   Aboard (Type/Design of Sailboat)

204
Bareboat Cruising Instructor

AFFIX SEAL HERE

Provisional Certification
for three (3) months
until seal is affixed

_____
Date

_____
ASA Instructor   Instructor Number

_____
ASA Certification Facility   Aboard (Type/Design of Sailboat)

205
Coastal Navigation Instructor

AFFIX SEAL HERE

Provisional Certification
for three (3) months
until seal is affixed

_____
Date

_____
ASA Instructor   Instructor Number

_____
ASA Certification Facility

INSTRUCTOR CERTIFICATIONS

THIS IS TO CERTIFY THAT:

Name

has successfully achieved the following ASA Instructor Standards:

206
Advanced Coastal Cruising Instructor

AFFIX SEAL HERE

Provisional Certification for three (3) months until seal is affixed

Date

ASA Instructor Instructor Number

ASA Certification Facility Aboard (Type/Design of Sailboat)

207
Celestial Navigation Instructor

AFFIX SEAL HERE

Provisional Certification for three (3) months until seal is affixed

Date

ASA Instructor Instructor Number

ASA Certification Facility

208
Offshore Passagemaking Instructor

AFFIX SEAL HERE

Provisional Certification for three (3) months until seal is affixed

Date

ASA Instructor Instructor Number

ASA Certification Facility Aboard (Type/Design of Sailboat)

INSTRUCTOR CERTIFICATIONS

THIS IS TO CERTIFY THAT:

___
Name

has successfully achieved the following ASA Instructor Standards:

210
Basic Small Boat Sailing Instructor

AFFIX SEAL HERE

Provisional Certification for three (3) months until seal is affixed

___
Date

___
ASA Instructor | Instructor Number

___
ASA Certification Facility | Aboard (Type/Design of Sailboat)

214
Cruising Catamaran Sailing Instructor

AFFIX SEAL HERE

Provisional Certification for three (3) months until seal is affixed

___
Date

___
ASA Instructor | Instructor Number

___
ASA Certification Facility | Aboard (Type/Design of Sailboat)

___
___
___

AFFIX SEAL HERE

Provisional Certification for three (3) months until seal is affixed

___
Date

___
ASA Instructor | Instructor Number

___
ASA Certification Facility | Aboard (Type/Design of Sailboat)

Instructor Endorsement Requirements

Instructors who hold valid credentials as listed below and who pass an Endorsement exam are generally authorized to certify the corresponding Student Endorsement. Docking Endorsement Instructor Certification also requires a skills evaluation by an Instructor Evaluator. See the 'Student Endorsements' section near the beginning of this Logbook for more information about Endorsements.

BASIC CELESTIAL NAVIGATION INSTRUCTOR (217)

PREREQUISITES:
- Coastal Navigation Instructor (205)

REQUIREMENTS:
- Minimum score of 90% on the Basic Celestial Navigation Endorsement Examination

AUTHORIZED TO CERTIFY:
- Basic Celestial Navigation Endorsement (117)

DOCKING ENDORSEMENT INSTRUCTOR (218)

PREREQUISITES:
- Basic Coastal Cruising Instructor (203)

REQUIREMENTS:
- Successful completion of the Docking Endorsement Examination and a practical skills exam.

AUTHORIZED TO CERTIFY:
- Docking Endorsement (118)

MARINE WEATHER ENDORSEMENT INSTRUCTOR (219)

PREREQUISITES:
- Basic Keelboat Instructor (201)

REQUIREMENTS:
- Minimum score of 90% on the Marine Weather Endorsement Examination

AUTHORIZED TO CERTIFY:
- Marine Weather Endorsement (119)

RADAR ENDORSEMENT INSTRUCTOR (ASA 220)

PREREQUISITES:
- Prerequisites: Coastal Navigation Instructor (ASA 205).

REQUIREMENTS:
- Miniumum score of 90% on the Radar Endorsement Examination

AUTHORIZED TO CERTIFY:
- Radar Endorsement (120)

Instructor Endorsements

Instructors who acquire the following Instructor Endorsement Seals are then authorized to teach the corresponding Student Endorsements. See also Student Endorsement Seals on pages 17-18, Student Endorsement Standards on pages 62-70, and Instructor Endorsement Standards on pages 81-82.

THIS IS TO CERTIFY THAT:

Name

has successfully achieved the following ASA STANDARDS:

	AFFIX SEAL HERE Provisional Certification for three (3) months until seal is affixed
Date	
ASA Instructor	Instructor Number
ASA Certification Facility	Aboard (Type/Design of Sailboat)

217 **Basic** **Celestial** **Endorsement** **Instructor**	AFFIX SEAL HERE Provisional Certification for three (3) months until seal is affixed
Date	
ASA Instructor	Instructor Number
ASA Certification Facility	

INSTRUCTOR ENDORSEMENTS

THIS IS TO CERTIFY THAT:

_____
Name

has successfully achieved the following ASA STANDARDS:

218
Docking Endorsement Instructor

AFFIX SEAL HERE

Provisional Certification
for three (3) months
until seal is affixed

_____
Date

_____
ASA Instructor   Instructor Number

_____
ASA Certification Facility   Aboard (Type/Design of Sailboat)

219
Marine Weather Endorsement Instructor

AFFIX SEAL HERE

Provisional Certification
for three (3) months
until seal is affixed

_____
Date

_____
ASA Instructor   Instructor Number

_____
ASA Certification Facility

220
Radar Endorsement Instructor

AFFIX SEAL HERE

Provisional Certification
for three (3) months
until seal is affixed

_____
Date

_____
ASA Instructor   Instructor Number

_____
ASA Certification Facility

Instructor Evaluator

The Instructor Evaluator (IE) Certification is the highest level in the ASA Certification System. IE's are responsible for ensuring that candidates seeking to become Certified ASA Instructors possess the professional, teaching and sailing skills necessary to safely instruct students according to the ASA Standards.

IE Certification Standards

PREREQUISITES:
- Minimum 25 years of age
- Valid Merchant Mariner Credential:
  - Operator of Uninspected Passenger Vessels (OUPV) with Sail Endorsement, or
  - Master with Sail Endorsement
- Minimum of one year since having attained Advanced Coastal Cruising Instructor Certification (206)
- Active teaching for a minimum of three years
- Minimum of one year teaching with an ASA Affiliate School
- Minimum score of 90% on all ASA examinations
- Possess excellent sailing abilities as demonstrated at previous IQCs
- Approval by the IE Council

REQUIREMENTS:
- Successful completion of an Instructor Evaluator Qualification Clinic (IEQC)
- Exhibit maturity, open-mindedness and control necessary to make tough decisions about IQC Candidates and support these decisions with constructive criticism
- Possess strong organizational abilities and be committed to spend 20 hours in preparation for an IQC

Instructor Evaluator Certification

See page 83 for IE Certification requirements.

THIS IS TO CERTIFY THAT:

Name

has successfully achieved the following ASA Instructor Standards:

211 **Instructor Evaluator**	AFFIX SEAL HERE Provisional Certification for three (3) months until seal is affixed
Date	

ASA Instructor — Instructor Number

ASA Certification Facility — Aboard (Type/Design of Sailboat)

SAILING LOG

Sailing Log (Record of major sailing experience)

DATES Leave & Arrive	TIME Leave & Arrive	LOCATION Origin, Destination Leave & Arrive	VESSEL NAME Size, LOA or Tonnage, Type	DAYS Onboard	DISTANCE Logged	NIGHT Hours (Watch)	DETAILS OF VOYAGE Crew Position, Weather, Special Duties, Incidents, etc.	CERTIFYING Signature

Students can copy blank pages to add to their Log entries. ASA also has an iPhone app for logging sailing experience.

SAILING LOG

Sailing Log (Record of major sailing experience)

DATES Leave & Arrive	TIME Leave & Arrive	LOCATION Origin, Destination Leave & Arrive	VESSEL NAME Size, LOA or Tonnage, Type	DAYS Onboard	DISTANCE Logged	NIGHT Hours (Watch)	DETAILS OF VOYAGE Crew Position, Weather, Special Duties, Incidents, etc.	CERTIFYING Signature

Students can copy blank pages to add to their Log entries. ASA also has an iPhone app for logging sailing experience.

SAILING LOG

Sailing Log (Record of major sailing experience)

DATES Leave & Arrive	TIME Leave & Arrive	LOCATION Origin, Destination Leave & Arrive	VESSEL NAME Size, LOA or Tonnage, Type	DAYS Onboard	DISTANCE Logged	NIGHT Hours (Watch)	DETAILS OF VOYAGE Crew Position, Weather, Special Duties, Incidents, etc.	CERTIFYING Signature

Students can copy blank pages to add to their Log entries. ASA also has an iPhone app for logging sailing experience.

SAILING LOG

Sailing Log (Record of major sailing experience)

DATES Leave & Arrive	TIME Leave & Arrive	LOCATION Origin, Destination Leave & Arrive	VESSEL NAME Size, LOA or Tonnage, Type	DAYS Onboard	DISTANCE Logged	NIGHT Hours (Watch)	DETAILS OF VOYAGE Crew Position, Weather, Special Duties, Incidents, etc.	CERTIFYING Signature

Students can copy blank pages to add to their Log entries. ASA also has an iPhone app for logging sailing experience.

SAILING LOG

Sailing Log (Record of major sailing experience)

DATES Leave & Arrive	TIME Leave & Arrive	LOCATION Origin, Destination Leave & Arrive	VESSEL NAME Size, LOA or Tonnage, Type	DAYS Onboard	DISTANCE Logged	NIGHT Hours (Watch)	DETAILS OF VOYAGE Crew Position, Weather, Special Duties, Incidents, etc.	CERTIFYING Signature

Students can copy blank pages to add to their Log entries. ASA also has an iPhone app for logging sailing experience.

Sailing Log (Record of major sailing experience)

DATES Leave & Arrive	TIME Leave & Arrive	LOCATION Origin, Destination Leave & Arrive	VESSEL NAME Size, LOA or Tonnage, Type	DAYS Onboard	DISTANCE Logged	NIGHT Hours (Watch)	DETAILS OF VOYAGE Crew Position, Weather, Special Duties, Incidents, etc.	CERTIFYING Signature

Students can copy blank pages to add to their Log entries. ASA also has an iPhone app for logging sailing experience.

SAILING LOG

Sailing Log (Record of major sailing experience)

DATES Leave & Arrive	TIME Leave & Arrive	LOCATION Origin, Destination Leave & Arrive	VESSEL NAME Size, LOA or Tonnage, Type	DAYS Onboard	DISTANCE Logged	NIGHT Hours (Watch)	DETAILS OF VOYAGE Crew Position, Weather, Special Duties, Incidents, etc.	CERTIFYING Signature

Students can copy blank pages to add to their Log entries. ASA also has an iPhone app for logging sailing experience.

Sailing Log (Record of major sailing experience)

DATES Leave & Arrive	TIME Leave & Arrive	LOCATION Origin, Destination Leave & Arrive	VESSEL NAME Size, LOA or Tonnage, Type	DAYS Onboard	DISTANCE Logged	NIGHT Hours (Watch)	DETAILS OF VOYAGE Crew Position, Weather, Special Duties, Incidents, etc.	CERTIFYING Signature

Students can copy blank pages to add to their Log entries. ASA also has an iPhone app for logging sailing experience.

SAILING LOG

Sailing Log (Record of major sailing experience)

DATES Leave & Arrive	TIME Leave & Arrive	LOCATION Origin, Destination Leave & Arrive	VESSEL NAME Size, LOA or Tonnage, Type	DAYS Onboard	DISTANCE Logged	NIGHT Hours (Watch)	DETAILS OF VOYAGE Crew Position, Weather, Special Duties, Incidents, etc.	CERTIFYING Signature

Students can copy blank pages to add to their Log entries. ASA also has an iPhone app for logging sailing experience.

SAILING LOG

Sailing Log (Record of major sailing experience)

DATES Leave & Arrive	TIME Leave & Arrive	LOCATION Origin, Destination Leave & Arrive	VESSEL NAME Size, LOA or Tonnage, Type	DAYS Onboard	DISTANCE Logged	NIGHT Hours (Watch)	DETAILS OF VOYAGE Crew Position, Weather, Special Duties, Incidents, etc.	CERTIFYING Signature

Students can copy blank pages to add to their Log entries. ASA also has an iPhone app for logging sailing experience.